CICELY'S SECRET

BY SUSAN BLACKABY

Celebration Press
Pearson Learning Group

CONTENTS

CHAPTER 1

"CICELY! CICELY!"

Cicely looked out the classroom window. The sky was a deep, bright blue. Puffy white clouds were drifting behind the canyon spires. It was a perfect day for a bike ride up the steep, winding canyon trails.

Cicely closed one eye and squinted at the ridge where it met the sky. She traced the edge of the ridge in the air with her pencil. She imagined that she was riding behind her dad. They would head up the canyon behind the ridge right there on the left. They would ride along for about a mile.

Then just beyond the second ridge, they would reach a sharp turn where the trail met up with the creek. They would stop right there and have a picnic on their favorite big, flat rock. They would dangle their feet over the edge of the rock and into the water. It was so cold that it made your toes sting, but it felt good on a hot day. The rock was Cicely's favorite place in the whole world.

Just then Cicely heard her name. Her brain snapped back to her books and her fourth-grade classroom.

"What?" she said. Her voice seemed to ring out in the stillness.

All around her, her classmates' heads were bent over their papers. The clock ticked quietly. Ms. Trancos was checking spelling tests at her desk at the front of the room. She peered at Cicely over her half glasses.

"What is it, Cicely?" she said.

Cicely felt kind of confused. What were they doing, again? Then she remembered; they were solving word problems. "Never mind. Sorry."

Ms. Trancos shook her head and went back to her work. Cicely looked down at her paper and read the first problem.

There are 19 slices in a loaf of bread. If 16 children want 2 sandwiches and 4 children want 1 1/2 sandwiches, how many loaves of bread will you need?

"I wonder what kind of sandwiches they are," thought Cicely. "The way I make toasted cheese takes just one slice of bread. Why would a loaf have 19 slices? Are you supposed to count the two end pieces? Nobody wants a sandwich made out of end pieces, so maybe there are really just 17 slices in a loaf."

Cicely twirled her bangs around her finger. She sighed. Then she was sure she heard someone say her name again.

"Cicely."

She looked around the classroom. Everyone was working on the math sheet. Tom was making a big smudge with his eraser; Lauren was fiddling with her pencil; Rico was tugging on his ear. No one seemed to be trying to get her attention.

"Cicely."

There it was again, a soft whisper. It sounded like the rustle of tissue paper in a box. It was coming from the science center.

"Cicely. Cicely."

Cicely looked at the terrarium on the science center shelf. Inside, the classroom snake, Siesta, was nodding her head and flicking out her tongue. Cicely squealed in surprise.

"What is it now, Cicely?" said Ms. Trancos.

Cicely felt very strange. She could hear the snake talking to her!

Aloud she said, "I'm sorry, Ms. Trancos, I … I … Look! Siesta!" She pointed at the snake.

Everyone in the room
scrambled over the desks to peer into
the terrarium. Siesta twisted her way out
of her cardboard box. Her head waved from
side to side; her bright eyes gleamed.

"Cicely," hissed Siesta. "Listen. Listen."

Cicely stared, amazed. Siesta's tongue flicked,
but no one else seemed to notice that a snake
was speaking perfect English. They were just
excited to see the snake again.

"All right, all right," said Ms. Trancos. "Calm
down, everyone. Our friend Siesta is awake. She
is coming out of her winter hibernation."

"She's probably really hungry," said Tom.

"May we feed her?" asked Kit.

"Mr. Brock is in charge of feeding her before
he locks up at night. We'll tell him that Siesta is
hungry, but right now it's important to review
the reptile rules. What is rule number one?"

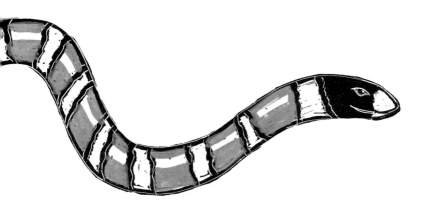

As the class went over the rules posted on the board, Cicely kept her eyes glued on Siesta. She had burrowed back down into the wood shavings, but her head was poking out. She seemed to be staring back at Cicely.

Ms. Trancos said to Cicely, "You seem to be especially interested in Siesta, Cicely. Maybe you'd like to find out more about the natural habitat of the Arizona mountain kingsnake and report to the class."

Cicely had been only half listening; she just nodded.

CHAPTER 2

DISTRACTED

When the recess bell rang, the class filed out into the sunshine. Ms. Trancos called to Cicely.

"You seem kind of distracted today," said Ms. Trancos. She put her hand on Cicely's shoulder. "You should go out and get some fresh air."

"Okay," said Cicely. "I just need to put on my jacket. I'll be right out."

When Cicely came out of the coat room, Ms. Trancos was gone. She went over to the terrarium, leaned down, and looked at Siesta.

Cicely really felt kind of silly, but she said, "Siesta, did you say something to me?"

"Yessss," hissed Siesta. "Siesta seeks assistance."

Cicely gripped the shelf. She could feel her heart thumping in her chest.

"What is it?" she whispered.

"Siesta seeks sky," Siesta whispered back.

Cicely looked out the window. The sun shone on the rock face of the canyon.

"You want sunshine?" asked Cicely.

"Yes," replied Siesta.

Cicely understood exactly how Siesta felt. Cicely couldn't imagine not being able to explore outdoors! "Poor Siesta," she thought. "This is no place for a snake to live."

"You want freedom?" continued Cicely.

Siesta closed her eyes. "Yes. Exactly," she hissed.

The bell rang, and Cicely scooted back to her desk. She was thinking hard about Siesta. Ms. Trancos had to say her name three times to get her attention.

"Cicely," Ms. Trancos said, "try to focus. We need to get back to our math lesson now. How many slices of bread will you need?"

Cicely stared at the numbers on her paper.

"Seventy-six," hissed Siesta.

"Seventy-six," said Cicely.

"Excellent," said Ms. Trancos.

"Excellent," hissed Siesta.

For the rest of the day, Cicely could barely concentrate. It was hard to ignore Siesta. At three o'clock Cicely grabbed her backpack.

"Cicely, save Siesta," hissed the snake.

"How?" whispered Cicely.

"Sneak Siesta out," the reptile hissed.

Cicely reached out for the latch on the little door. Then she stopped.

"I can't do it," she said. "It's not right. Something terrible might happen. What else can I do?" said Cicely.

"See Sam Cisneros," replied Siesta.

Sam Cisneros was a kid in her brother's grade. Cicely had heard that he was working on a nature park project in the canyon, although she wasn't exactly sure what that was.

"Please see Sam," Siesta repeated.

"I'll try," Cicely whispered.

"Promise," hissed Siesta.

"I promise!" said Cicely.

Cicely waved goodbye to Siesta. Then she looked around and saw that Ms. Trancos was watching her.

Ms. Trancos stopped Cicely at the door. "Are you sure you are all right?" she asked Cicely. "You seemed kind of nervous today."

"I'm fine," Cicely said. "And the project will be fun." She smiled and ducked out the door.

When Cicely got home, she ran up the stairs and banged on her brother's bedroom door.

"Emilio!" she called. "Emilio!"

Emilio was thirteen. Cicely was not supposed to bug him when he was with his friends, but she needed help.

"Emilio! Let me in," Cicely called.

The door opened. Emilio and his friend Alan were working on a model of a mining town for Emilio's train set. They had been at it for weeks.

"Who let you out of the game preserve?" asked Emilio.

"I need to get hold of Sam Cisneros," said Cicely.

"What for?" asked Emilio.

"That is a good question," thought Cicely. "Do I say, 'Siesta told me to find him'?" Her hands were sweaty.

"Oh, I need information about, you know, local snakes," she said. "That's right—Arizona mountain kingsnakes—like Siesta, the snake in our classroom."

"Ss-ss-ss-sam is the man for that," said Alan. "He was nuts about that dumb snake."

"Sam was always hanging around Siesta," said Emilio, "and he wanted to set her free. He drove Ms. Trancos crazy when we were in her class."

"Interesting," said Cicely, trying to sound breezy. "I wonder where Sam is right now."

"He's probably at the library," said Alan. "He volunteers there on Tuesdays after school."

Cicely bounded out of the room and headed for the front door.

"Your sister is so weird," said Alan.

"Tell me about it," said Emilio.

Cicely slipped on her helmet and hopped on her bike. She took off for the bike path that wound into town.

CHAPTER 3

SEEKING HELP

When Cicely got to the library, she spotted Sam kneeling down to shelve books in the children's section.

"Excuse me," she whispered. "You're Sam, right?"

He turned and nodded. "Well, I've been asked to deliver an urgent message."

Sam stood up. "What message?" he asked.

"I can't tell you here," whispered Cicely. "It's from Siesta—Siesta at Ridgeview School."

Sam steered Cicely to the door. "I have to take a quick break, Ms. Bridges," he said as they passed the librarian. "I'll be right back."

When they got outside, Sam looked around to make sure no one could hear them.

"Who are you, and what are you talking about?" he demanded.

"My name is Cicely. I'm Emilio Santana's sister," said Cicely in a rush. "I'm in Ms. Trancos's class. Siesta woke up today and talked to me. She asked me to find you."

"She asked you to find me?" Sam's serious face broke into a grin. "So somebody else can hear her?"

Cicely smiled nervously. "She begged me to set her free, and I think she wants you to help me. What should I tell her?"

"Tell her we'll think of a plan," said Sam, "and that I won't let her down this time."

That night after dinner Cicely was working on her report and drawing a picture of Siesta living in the wild when the telephone rang.

"Hi, Cicely," said Sam. "I forgot to warn you. Siesta will try to get you mixed up during class. She'll give you the wrong answers."

"She gave me the right answer today during math class," said Cicely.

"That was today," said Sam. "Remember, she's been in fourth grade for years, so she's bored stiff. You have to be careful."

"Okay," said Cicely, "I'll be careful. Bye."

CHAPTER 4

THE PLAN TAKES SHAPE

The next morning Dad drove Cicely to school.

"Dad, what's the nature park project?" she asked.

"A group of folks headed by the Cisneros family want to create a nature park outside of town," said Dad. "The property goes way up into the canyon. One of the old ranchers donated it to the city."

"What are they going to do with the land?" asked Cicely.

"Well, it's had cattle grazing on it for years," said Dad. "They plan to restore it with sagebrush and other native plants. The restored habitat will attract wildlife, and the animals will be protected."

"If an Arizona mountain kingsnake lived there, would it be protected?" asked Cicely.

"Well, it would be protected from people," said Dad. "It would still be fair game for hawks and coyotes and other predators, of course."

"Protected doesn't mean completely safe then, does it?" asked Cicely.

"No, not completely," said Dad. He pulled the car up to let Cicely off by the flagpole. "If we are free this weekend, we could ride out there and take a look," he said.

"That sounds great, Dad," said Cicely, giving him an extra hug.

Cicely was the first one to arrive in the classroom, and she headed straight for the terrarium. Siesta was nowhere to be seen. Had she escaped? Cicely tried to see into the tissue box. She gently tapped the glass with her fingernails.

"Siesta," she said softly, "I saw Sam Cisneros."

Cicely watched the wood shavings move and shift. The red and black and white stripes of Siesta's sleek body emerged into view.

"Cicely, you saw Sam?" Siesta stared and flicked her tongue in and out.

"Yes," said Cicely. "Sam said he'd help. We'll think of a plan; we won't let you down."

"Super," hissed Siesta happily. Then she disappeared into her shavings again.

After math class Cicely raised her hand. "Ms. Trancos," she asked, "may we take Siesta outside?"

"I'm sure everyone would love to, Cicely, but it's too dangerous. She might get loose."

"Then she'd be free," said Cicely.

"She'd be a free lunch," said Rico, making his hand into a dive-bombing bird.

"Siesta can take care of herself," said Cicely, "and besides, she has friends."

"We're her friends, Cicely, and she'll be safe and sound right here," said Ms. Trancos.

"She's been here so long she's gotten used to living here," said Kit.

"How could you ever get used to being trapped like that?" Cicely felt angry and frustrated. "She can barely move in there."

"She's just lazy from her big meal last night," said Ms. Trancos. "She'll probably come out and move around this afternoon. In the meantime let's get started on our social studies."

"But Ms. Trancos," Cicely protested, "doesn't Siesta need fresh air and sunshine just the way we do?"

"Cicely," said Ms. Trancos, "unless you plan to get a job as a snake charmer, I suggest you get your mind off Siesta and pay attention to what we are studying. Please get out your social studies books. Who can remind us what the capital of Texas is?"

"Osprey," hissed Siesta.

"Osprey," said Cicely.

Ms. Trancos raised her eyebrows. "An osprey is a bird of prey, Cicely, but thank you for your input. The capital of Texas is Austin. And what important energy product comes from Texas?"

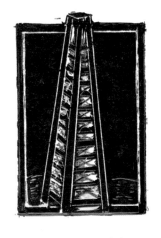

"Steak sauce," hissed Siesta.

"Steak sauce," said Cicely.

Everyone laughed. Cicely thought she could hear Siesta laughing, too. It sounded like tearing paper.

Ms. Trancos sighed. "Cicely, we will be delighted to hear you read about drilling for

oil. I'm sure you'll find it very informative. Begin on page 125."

"Disaster!" hissed Siesta.

"Very funny," Cicely whispered.

That evening, Sam phoned again.

"I've got an idea," he said. "You could write up a petition saying that Siesta should have a new home at the nature park. Then you can get the kids at school to sign it. Tell them it's not healthy for Siesta to be all cooped up indoors."

"I don't know if I can persuade them," said Cicely. "They think Siesta is a pet."

"She isn't a pet. She's a wild animal, and she deserves a better life than being caged in a classroom at Ridgeview School."

"I'll do my best," said Cicely.

Cicely thought a while and then carefully printed out a statement for the petition. *We the undersigned believe Siesta deserves her freedom as a wild creature.* She attached the sheet to a clipboard and put her signature on the top line.

The next day Cicely passed the clipboard around to her classmates, but she couldn't get any signatures. She felt discouraged. On top of that, Siesta was alert and full of mischief all day.

Even though Sam had warned Cicely, Siesta had a way of making things pop into Cicely's head and right out her mouth. It was embarrassing and dangerous. Also, whenever Cicely talked with Siesta, Ms. Trancos seemed to be watching them.

"Siesta, settle down," whispered Cicely.

After lunch Ms. Trancos said it was "Time to G.A.B." That meant "time to get a book" for free reading. The classroom was quiet except for Siesta's nonstop chatter.

"Cicely," she hissed. "Sam says that sand is sensational. Is it? Siesta wants to slither on a sea of sand. Cicely, speak to Siesta."

"No," whispered Cicely.

"Siesta insists," she hissed.

"No," said Cicely.

"Cicely," said Ms. Trancos, " 'Time to G.A.B.' does not mean time to gab. What are you reading?"

Cicely had no idea. The book she held was upside down. She had not been reading it at all.

"*The Summer Season*," hissed Siesta.

"*The Summer Season*," said Cicely.

"What is it about?" asked Ms. Trancos.

"Ice skating," hissed Siesta.

"Ice skating." The second Cicely said it, she knew it was ridiculous. Ms. Trancos was staring at her. "Did I say ice skating? I meant baseball." Cicely turned her book rightside up and started reading. She hoped Ms. Trancos would not ask any more questions. She also hoped that Siesta would keep quiet.

"Ice skating in summer," Siesta giggled. "Cicely is so silly."

At the end of the day, Cicely quickly put her things in her back pack. She was still upset about Siesta's teasing, but then she thought, "Poor Siesta didn't have anything more interesting to do. And besides, I didn't have to repeat what she said."

She quickly said goodbye to Siesta. "I'm going to meet Sam. Sit tight."

Cicely shared a seat on the school bus with Kit. "Scoot over a little, please," complained Kit. "I'm all cramped up. These seats are torture if you have long legs like mine."

"You're like Siesta," said Cicely, "all curled up like a pretzel. Siesta is almost three feet long, but she doesn't have room to stretch out," said Cicely. She spread her arms about a yard wide.

"Get out of here," said Kit in disbelief.

She thought for a few minutes. Then she said, "Where's that petition? I think I'll sign it."

We the undersigned believe Siesta deserves her freedom.
Cicely
Kit

31

Sam met Cicely at the bus stop. "How did it go today?" he asked.

"I fell right into Siesta's traps," said Cicely, "and I only got one signature on the petition."

"Don't worry," said Sam. "One signature is a good start."

They walked up to Cicely's house and through a side door into the kitchen. Sam greeted Cicely's mom.

"Hi, Mrs. Santana. Remember me?"

"Of course I do, Sam," said Cicely's mom, taking a bag of popcorn out of the microwave. "It's nice to see you. Emilio should be home soon."

"Sam's here to see me, Mom," said Cicely.

 "We're working on this snake project. It's kind of complicated. Anyway, we're going to work outside." Cicely took the bag of popcorn and some juice.

Sam and Cicely went into the yard. They climbed a ladder to a high platform hidden by the branches of a large pine tree. The platform made a porch around a little  three-sided shelter with a slanted roof. Inside were some benches and a table made from an old foot locker.

"This place is fantastic," said Sam.

"Yeah, I love it up here. All my stuff is in the trunk, and the benches push together to make a little bed. I can see the whole world during the day and the whole universe at night."

"The view is amazing," said Sam. He pointed out across the valley. "You can see where the trail goes up into South Canyon. Who built this place?"

"Emilio and Alan built it," said Cicely. "They'll do about anything to get rid of me, so they made me my own little habitat. Emilio calls it my game preserve."

"Do you think they'd help us build a game preserve for Siesta?" asked Sam.

"They might. Does this mean we've got a plan?" asked Cicely.

"Maybe Emilio could help design a special enclosure for Siesta at the nature park. Then we could move Siesta there. She'd have plenty of room to slither around, and she'd be in her natural environment. She could be part of an education program at the park. We could even have other snakes there, too," said Sam.

"Maybe Ms. Trancos could be in charge of setting up the program, and then she might change her mind about letting Siesta live there," suggested Cicely.

"Great idea!" said Sam, smiling broadly. "You keep working on that petition, and I'll ask my parents to speak to the nature park planning group about Ms. Trancos. I bet they'll be glad to put her in charge of the education program." Sam gazed out over the valley. "This just might work," he said.

CHAPTER 5

PERSUADING OTHERS

The next day Cicely told Siesta about the plan. Siesta was very upset. She coiled up and flicked her tongue in and out.

"Simply free Siesta," she hissed. "Slide Siesta inside your sleeve! Sneak Siesta outside!"

"We've been over that already. I can't just take you and let you go," said Cicely crossly. "It isn't right, and besides, you wouldn't be safe. You have to trust me. Sam and I will get you out of here."

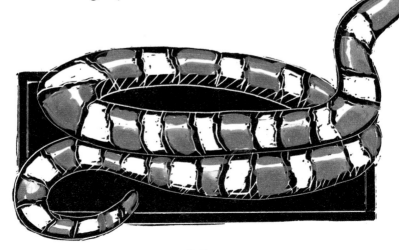

That afternoon Cicely presented her report on the kingsnake's natural habitat to the class. Afterward she had her petition ready for her classmates to sign if she could just persuade them to change their minds.

"I don't think it is good to keep Siesta away from her natural habitat," she said.

No one really seemed interested.

"Listen," said Cicely. "How would you feel if you had to stay in this classroom day and night? How would you feel if you couldn't play basketball or go swimming or even stretch your legs out straight? I know how I would feel if I couldn't go outside or ride my bike up to the creek. Think about how Siesta feels. She needs her freedom."

"Siesta seeks sand. Siesta seeks sky," Siesta coached Cicely.

"She seeks sand and sky," said Cicely. "If we care about her, we should think about her needs first."

"That's ridiculous, Cicely," said Tom. "She has the perfect life right here at Ridgeview School. She has plenty of shavings and a nice tissue box. Mr. Brock brings her yummy meals."

"Yummy?" questioned Cicely. "Suppose you had to eat the same cold food for every meal for the rest of your life. Would you like that?"

"Well, no, I wouldn't like it, and I guess maybe Siesta would like a little variety once in a while, too. Okay, I get your point. I'll sign your petition."

Tom reached for the clipboard.

Later that day Cicely and Lauren were working in the classroom art center. They were drawing their family trees.

"You have a big family," said Cicely.

"I like being in a big family," said Lauren. "I'd get lonesome without a bunch of people around the house all the time."

"Siesta never gets to see her own family," said Cicely.

"That seems sad. I wonder how she feels about it?" replied Lauren.

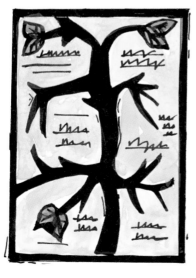

"She's miserable," said Cicely. "Just look at her."

"I am looking at her," said Lauren. "She seems to be shedding her skin."

"That is exactly my point. She's a grown-up snake. She needs to be around other snakes. She's all alone in our classroom."

"I guess I never thought about it from Siesta's point of view," said Lauren.

Cicely held out the clipboard, and Lauren signed. Cicely got four more signatures during noon recess. She reported her progress to Siesta after lunch.

"So slow," hissed Siesta.

"Slow and steady," said Cicely.

That afternoon Ms. Trancos was teaching a science lesson about erosion. She explained how the canyons had been slowly worn down by wind and rain.

"This would be so much easier if we could actually see it," said Cicely. "It's kind of hard to picture what you mean."

"You're right," said Ms. Trancos, "and we do have incredible examples of erosion right here. Thousands of years ago this valley was completely under water. Shells and the skeletons of ancient sea creatures are embedded in the rock face of South Canyon. The erosion has made these fossils visible."

"Wow," said Rico, "I didn't know that. We should take a field trip over there to see them."

"As a matter of fact," said Ms. Trancos, "I am going to be setting up an outdoor classroom at the new nature park in the canyon."

"An outdoor classroom sounds neat," said Cicely. "It'd be the perfect place to keep Siesta!"

Ms. Trancos shook her head. "I'm sorry, Cicely. I think that Siesta is too tame. If she were released into the wild, she wouldn't know how to survive."

"Sam says he and my brother, Emilio, can make a safe spot at the nature park where Siesta could get used to being on her own," said Cicely.

"You must mean Sam Cisneros. He was always interested in snakes, too," said Ms. Trancos.

"You know, this sounds like a pretty good idea after all, Cicely," said Rico, reaching for the clipboard. "My sister is working on that project. She calls it a living museum."

"Let me take a look at that petition, Cicely," said Ms. Trancos. Cicely passed her the clipboard. Ms. Trancos read the statement and counted down the list of names signed below it. She smiled and nodded her head.

"Success! Success!" hissed Siesta.

"All the students seem serious about seeing Siesta set free now, Ms. Trancos. There must be some way to set up a special safe place for her," said Cicely.

"Cicely, you sound just like Siesta!" laughed Kit.

"Oh, brother." Tom rolled his eyes. Then in a soft voice he said, "Siesta! Cicely is going to save you!"

Cicely laughed nervously. She glanced at Ms. Trancos and was relieved to see that she was laughing with the rest of the group. She didn't seem to have noticed any unusual communication going on between Cicely and Siesta. Cicely's secret was safe.

"Say something snappy," encouraged Siesta.

"As I was saying," said Cicely, "my brother can help. He can build a safe spot for Siesta. She can live there until she gets used to her surroundings. We can feed her there, too. That way if she can't hunt, at least she won't starve."

"Visit! Visit!" hissed Siesta.

"Also," Cicely continued, "we'll be able to visit Siesta as often as we want to and observe her in a more natural habitat."

"Is it possible?" asked Siesta.

"It is possible," said Cicely. "We just have to agree that freedom is the best thing for Siesta."

"That was quite a speech," said Ms. Trancos. "I'm impressed with the work and thought you have put into this. When do you think Emilio and Sam can complete a habitat design?"

"Instantly," hissed Siesta.

"They can do it instantly," said Cicely.

"Next week will be just fine," said Ms. Trancos with a smile.

CHAPTER 6

A DREAM COMES TRUE

On a bright, clear Saturday morning, Cicely and her dad rode their bikes to the nature park. Cicely stopped at the enclosure near the outdoor classroom. Nylon netting surrounded the enclosure. Inside, there was a miniature miner's shack in the shade of some rocks. The sagebrush rippled in the breeze.

Sam and Ms. Trancos were inside the enclosure planting cactus. "Hey, Cicely," said Sam. He waved to Cicely's dad.

"How is my slithery friend?" Cicely asked.

"She has something to show you," said Sam, opening the door to let Cicely inside the enclosure.

Siesta gracefully moved over the sand, curling around the rocks and plants blocking her path. "Cicely," hissed Siesta, "see Siesta's nest!"

Cicely followed Siesta to the shack and peeked into the shadows. She counted six eggs in the nest.

"When will they hatch?" whispered Cicely.

"Six weeks," hissed Siesta. "So exciting!"

Cicely smiled at Siesta. Then Cicely looked at Sam.

"I'd say we have a special secret," said Sam.

"Yes, an awesome, special secret," agreed Cicely with a smile.